BULB RECRUITMENT HANDBOOK

Growing and caring for bulbs

BYRON MOUSER

Table of Contents

CHAPTER ONE

BULB RECRUITMENT

Growing and caring for bulbs

A bulb is a wonderful, self-contained plant package that is nearly foolproof. Every bulb conceals a fully formed plant embryo, including roots, leaves, and flowers. If you give the bulb the right care and nutrients, it will flourish. To get the most out of your bulbs in terms of blooming and growth, there are a few things you should keep in mind when planting them.

Start planting right away.

This weekend is the perfect time to plant bulbs, so go get some from the crisper or head to the nursery. Each bulb contains an entire embryonic plant, down to the roots, leaves, and flowers. The bulb can flourish in any suitable environment. Bulbs are one of the "requirements" mentioned. They can't be saved for later planting because they aren't seeds. Whether or not you plant bulbs, they will sprout.

There are many different ways to plant bulbs in the garden, including in beds, clumps, or containers. They need to be planted at the correct depth and orientation in the soil wherever you decide to grow them. The bulb needs to be planted deep enough so that it stays cool, but not so deep that its shoot can't make it to the surface before it runs out of energy. Planting bulbs at a depth equal to twice their width is a good rule of thumb, though the packaging will typically indicate the optimal planting depth (and this is the depth to the top of the bulb).

Consequently, a larger bulb necessitates a deeper planting location.

Tulips, when cultivated in containers, make lovely additions to patios, porches, and other outdoor spaces.

DEEPNESS AND DIRECTION

Both the depth and the direction in which a plant is planted are essential to its success. For the best results, plant your winter and spring flowering bulbs below ground. Bulbs should be planted at a depth that's twice their width, as a general rule. That's why it's important to plant larger bulbs at a deeper depth.

While larger bulbs like tulips, hyacinths, and daffodils should be planted several inches below the soil's surface, smaller bulbs like freesias, anemones, and crocuses should be set much closer to the soil's surface.

Because the bulb's roots develop at its base and its growing tip is located at its crown, orientation is also crucial. This piece must be oriented so that it faces the top of the soil. Some bulbs have an unusual shape that makes it harder to tell which end is the top and which is the bottom when planting.

When it comes to the anemone (Anemone coronaria), the pointy end goes down. The point of these corms, which is the root and not the growing tip, is positioned downward, giving them the appearance of chocolate drops. The strange corms of the ranunculus (Ranunculus asiaticus) have the appearance of claws, which can add to the bafflement. The roots, or "claws," are anchored at the base of the plant.

TROUBLESHOOTING

The stored energy of a bulb may be depleted if it is planted too deeply or the wrong way up. The bulb's roots develop from the bottom, while the plant's tiny growing tip is located at the very top.

If bulbs are planted too shallow, they will not thrive. They could be affected by the extreme heat or cold above ground, or eaten by predators or agitated by humans. All my daffodils were dug up by a flock of sulphur-crested cockatoos once. Even after scaring the birds away and replanting the bulbs with a thicker layer of mulch, many of them were too badly damaged to survive.

BULk LAMP INSTALLER

Dig a large hole and place your bulbs inside if you need to plant many bulbs at once. Or you could buy a bulb planter.

If you use this ingenious tool to dig out a small area of soil, you'll have plenty of room to set the bulb in its socket. With its helpful markings, you can easily find the optimal planting depth for any bulb. Once the bulb is in place, dump the soil from the scoop over it. You can find it in garden centers, hardware stores, or online from bulb retailers.

Popular spring bulbs, such as daffodils, start blooming in the winter and continue to do so in waves all the way into spring.

REDUCE SHRUGGING

Gardeners often have to deal with the unsightly, long, strappy leaves of bulbs until late spring or even early summer. You might be tempted to do a quick prune to make things look better, but doing so could reduce the plant's chances of flowering next year because its leaves are currently producing food for its growth.

There are a few options if you want to grow a lot of bulbs but don't want to deal with their unruly leaves. They are easily grown in containers and relocated to a less conspicuous location once the blooms have faded. It is also possible to let other plants in the garden take care of hiding the leaves of bulbs after they have finished flowering.

Growing quickly in the spring and filling in the gaps left by the bulbs, water-wise summer perennials like dianthus, yarrow, euphorbia, and candytuft, or annuals like marigolds and Californian poppy, do a fantastic job. Let the grasses around your bulb plantings grow as long as possible before mowing it in the early summer for a more natural meadow effect.

CHAPTER TWO

Instructions for Growing and Planting Spring-Blooming Bulbs

In many parts of the world, the arrival of spring is marked by the blooming of spring bulbs. Bulbs that bloom in the spring provide an eye-catching display while the rest of the garden is just emerging from its winter slumber. The best results will come from following these straightforward instructions when planting them.

When to Plant Bulbs for Spring Color

As a general rule, spring-flowering bulbs are planted in the fall. However, fall lasts for about 12 weeks, and the weather and soil conditions at the beginning of fall in late September and at the end of fall in late November are quite different.

The optimal planting time for bulbs is different for each variety and geographic location. If you want to know when to plant a certain species, you should consult the University Extension Service or a reputable local nursery. Planting daffodils in Minnesota is advised in September, but in Tennessee it's advised to wait until late November. To prevent them from sending up leaves too soon, tulips should be planted in November (before the ground freezes).

Waiting until air temperatures are consistently below 50 degrees Fahrenheit and soil temperatures are at or below 55 degrees Fahrenheit is a good strategy that works for most spring bulbs. If you live in a cold climate, you can plant spring-blooming bulbs even if the ground is frozen.

Many traditional spring bulbs, including daffodils, tulips, hyacinths, and crocuses, need a cold-chilling period of up to 16 weeks before they are ready to bloom in the spring, which is why they must be planted in the fall. But if you live in a place where winters rarely drop below 40 degrees Fahrenheit for an extended period, you may have trouble growing these bulbs unless you artificially chill them in the fridge for 10 to 12 weeks or buy them prechilled.

Those who garden in warmer climates but don't want to bother with artificially chilling bulbs should instead plant later-blooming bulbs like amaryllis, paperwhites, ranunculus, and anemones.

Ahead of Time:

Stay away from any bulbs that look moldy, soft, or withered. To a large extent, the size of the bulb determines the size of the flowers it produces. Less expensive bulbs often produce fewer or smaller blossoms due to their diminutive size. It's fine to keep the small bulblets when dividing an established group of bulbs, but keep in mind that it may be a couple of years before they are strong enough to produce flowers.

CHAPTER THREE

Materials Required

Instrumentation / Instruments

A Spade for the Garden

• Red pepper flakes or a hardware cloth (if needed for animal control)

Materials

Bulbs that bloom in the spring

Bone meal, a balanced fertilizer,

Instructions

1. Opt for an Appropriate Site

Bulbs are a type of plant that thrives in direct sunlight. A garden area's lack of sunlight during the warmer months shouldn't make you ignore it, though. It is safe to plant spring bulbs around or beneath the canopy of shade trees because they bloom before most deciduous trees have leaves. Avoid planting spring bulbs in the shade of a house, garage, or fence on the north side of your property.

Second, keep in mind some basic design principles

In order to achieve their full aesthetic potential, bulbs should be planted in dense drifts or clumps. Either dig a large hole and place a bunch of bulbs in it all at once, or just toss the bulbs into the air, dig holes, and plant them wherever they land. A more organic appearance can be achieved in the garden, according to some gardeners, by planting bulbs in odd numbers in clusters. Unless you want an artificial effect, planting in formal geometric rows isn't a good idea.

Third, Assess and Get the Ground Ready

Constantly moist soil is bad for bulbs because it promotes rot. During the summer, when the bulbs are dormant, this is especially true. Choose a planting spot that has good soil drainage not only during the summer but throughout the year. Soil conditions that are similar to those found in arid regions, like the Mediterranean or the mountains, are ideal for the growth of many spring bulbs.

There is no need to fertilize bulbs when planting them because they already contain the embryo of next year's flowers. Add a handful of bone meal or a balanced fertilizer to the planting hole if the soil is poor. Light fertilization of bulbs in the spring can aid in the development of next year's embryo.

Fourth, ensure proper planting depth.

Bulbs need to be planted at a depth equal to two to three times their eventual height. For daffodils, the standard recommendation is to plant them 6 to 8 inches deep; for bulbs measuring 2 inches from nose to base, plant them 4 to 6 inches deep. Planting bulbs at a shallower depth than recommended usually results in the bulbs growing deeper roots within a year or two.

5. Make sure the bulbs are upright

It's easy to tell which way is up and which way is down when it comes to many different types of light bulbs. When planting a bulb, make sure the pointed end is facing up because that is the stem. On the flatter, lower end of the bulb, you may even be able to see some shriveled, hair-like roots.

However, knowing which way is up isn't always easy. If that's the case, you can just plant the bulb on its side, and the stems should work their way up. In fact, bulbs planted in an upside-down position will typically still sprout and bloom, albeit a few days later.

Keep the Lights On!

Some rodents, such as squirrels and chipmunks, are well-known for stealing spring flowering bulbs. If you notice this happening, you can prevent further damage by covering the bulbs with a layer of chicken wire or hardware cloth before filling in the planting hole. The bulb stems and foliage can grow through these materials, but the bulbs will be protected from rodents.

To prevent rodents from destroying your bulbs during planting, you can also try adding a few pinches of red pepper flakes to the soil. You could also restrict yourself to daffodils and other bulbous flowering plants that are typically ignored by rodents and other animals.

Seven, Identify the Future Garden

After the bulb foliage has died back for the season, don't plant anything else there without first marking the area. A small wooden craft stick, a plant tag, or a decorative stone can serve as the marker. You could also make a garden plan that details where each set of bulbs goes.

Step Eight: Give Your Lights the Proper Amount of Water

After planting bulbs, water them right away to help the soil settle, eliminate air gaps, and kickstart the bulbs' root development. If there isn't a severe drought after the first watering, you should let nature take its course and stop watering.

Minimize or eliminate watering during the growing season. The majority of spring bulbs come from arid regions, so it's not wise to overwater them. During the fall and winter months, your bulbs will only need watering during extended dry spells. You ought to reap the benefits of your labor come spring.

CHAPTER FOUR

Use Appropriate Follow-Up Care

When the flowers have faded and the foliage has turned yellow and died, you can either pull it off or trim it down to the ground. Don't be tempted to trim away at the greenery just yet. The leaves must have sufficient photosynthesis time to produce food for the bulbs. When you prune your bulbs too early, the bulbs don't get the chance to store enough energy to produce flowers the following year.

Whenever Necessary, Split the Light Bulbs in Half 10

After a few years, the area where you planted your bulbs may be too crowded with the new plants it has spawned. Daffodils, in particular, fall into this category. Overcrowding could be to blame if your bulbs aren't flowering as profusely as they once did. Your bulbs can be divided when they enter their dormant period, typically right after the foliage has died back.

Don't procrastinate too long; dormancy is temporary. Pick out the largest and healthiest bulbs, then replant them at the appropriate distances. Throw away any bulbs that are too small or broken.

www.ingramcontent.com/pod-product-compliance
Lightning Source LLC
LaVergne TN
LVHW010511160826
845677LV00012B/2793

* 9 7 9 8 8 4 7 0 7 5 1 4 5 *